Veins

Veins

Poems by Larry Johnson

David Robert Books

Published by David Robert Books
P.O. Box 541106
Cincinnati, OH 45254-1106

ISBN: 9781934999691
LCCN: 2009937339

Poetry Editor: Kevin Walzer
Business Editor: Lori Jareo

Visit us on the web at www.davidrobertbooks.com

Acknowledgments

The author thanks the editors of the following publications where some of the poems in this volume appeared:

Anthology: A Collection of Poems from Mellen Poetry Press: "Frozen Danube"
Bayou: "Gottschalk in Peru," "Trajan at the Persian Gulf"
Chronicles: "Burton on Fernando Po," "Caesar in Parthia," "Jean Sibelius Bags a Soviet Plane, 1948," "Last Days of Juvenal"
Confluence: "Death of the Bat-Poet"
Folio: A Literary Journal: "New Moon"
Hellas: "Death of Caracalla"
The Hollins Critic: "To Lorca"
The Iowa Review: "Modern Poet and Calypso"
Kansas Quarterly: "Beginning," "When I Die"
Lips: "Agrippina"
The Little Review: "Egyptian Love Poem"
The Magnolia Quarterly: "Man Going," "Villanelle for the Greenhouse Effect"
The Maple Leaf Rag: "Pavane for a Dead Princess"
Mississippi Writers: Reflections of Childhood and Youth: "Near Eastabuchie, Mississippi," "Once"
National Forum: "For All Hostages"
Nebo: "For Yukio Mishima"
New Orleans Review: "Honey," "Red Skeletons of Herculaneum"
Paideuma: "In Memory of Ezra Pound"
Pebble: "Marcus Aurelius at the Colosseum"
Poem: "Earth"
Poetry Northwest: "Soliloquy Against McLuhan"
Sackbut Review: "Memory"
Southern Humanities Review: "Clodia"
Southern Poetry Anthology, Vol. II: Mississippi: "The

Capture of Weldon Kees," "For Jessica S.," "Red Skeletons
    of Herculaneum," "Sentry"
St. Andrews Review: "Morte d'Oscar"
Stone Country: "Camera Obscura"
The Texas Quarterly: "Cavafy Poem," "Near Eastabuchie,
    Mississippi," "*Tanous*"
Transatlantic Review: "Hadrian at Tivoli"
VQOnline: "Dream of Krakatoa"
Whiskey Island Magazine: "Withdrawal"

Thanks go to Dena White for love and encouragement and
to the late James Whitehead, the very best of teachers.

The author is also grateful to Allen Hoey, who reformatted
the book.

For Jack, Johnny, David, Kay, and John

—ἕτερος γὰρ αὐτὸς ὁ φίλος ἐστίν

Table of Contents

II Adrenalin Light

I

Adrenalin Night

(the present to 1821)

Man Going

What is on earth that tenses
in this silence
of a meteor sifting through Leo's flank
and Spica burning pearl
in the Virgin's thigh?

How may we see beyond this
long night of voices—
the crawling wave sucking up
the sand—
and the fire's flindering rust?

On deep hills, some man may feel
the moon's difference
in his thick fur coming . . .

Have we slashed through thinning skies
and earth's heavy pulp
only to pause and hear
the wind's edge retreating,
the rattle of dry beans?

Even old venom in the mouth
was spirited—
let us ease back to warm sand
and the sucking sea
and feed on ruins of strange fish.

The Capture of Weldon Kees

And so, Juan Robiños, after thirty years
The hand fell on your shoulder and you whirled,
Gazed into sungreen eyes, gold hair, and thought
My drowned daughter would have looked like this—
And there they were: tequila in one hand,
Books in the other, and lower, at khakied hips,
The nine-millimeter automatics. *The jazz!*
The jazz, you thought. It was all a trap.

Indeed it was—Coalcomán was not
A town for jazz, or anything but rum
And scrubby palm trees, cactus juice, and salt
Crusting over the sand like a glass's rim.
How many days had they played before you heard,
Before you came down this one street and found
The lime-painted cafe, and felt the chords
And entered—and why didn't you flee
At once, seeing the tall, tanless blonde
(Her virid oceans of eyes)—too haughty-clean
To be a tourist—and the little band
Too kempt, well-fed, their faces turned away
As they skreeled jazz outpristining your conceit.
Behaving like someone in your own poems
You ordered a drink and listened to the sax
Call you to ascend a desert of light
Toward dry, clear eternities . . . but then
You turned your back—and the hand clamped and held.
Magenta blood that Rimbaud strangled up

Before his death had crept for thirty years
Closer, each sand grain closer, and spread mind-wide
Until, transforming to a delicate hand,
It seeped into your shoulder. When it joined
Your veins it shrilled with a martyr's bliss.

The music ended while your terror grew
Into bewilderment—the band became
Six sinewed soldiers and the willowy girl.
They grinned for a second; frowned. She raised her glass
(Seagreen fingernails sliding slick around it),
Childlike, and spoke softly through Dovering teeth:
"Hello, Mr. Kees. Would you like one last sip?
The autographs can wait—we have to go."
"What . . ." you blurted. "I can't go anywhere."
(Were you speaking Spanish or English?) "Who are you?"
They smiled again—saw something in your eyes:
"Alcatraz is closed, Mr. Kees," she said.
I saw it sparkle as I cleared the rail . . .
"I am Juan Robiños," you rasped. "Cobalt blue,
My last sight was realms of cobalt blue."
She purred, "Yes, Mr. Robinson died, Mr. Kees.
He drowned in San Francisco Bay at last.
Maxfield Parrish outlived him: had you remained
In our world he might have outlived *you.*
We're here to take you home for trial now."
You thought—what kind of weird guerrilla band
With 1984 behind them now
(What *had* occurred in America these last years?)
Was this? Were those handcuffs at her belt?
Wide kohl-lined eyes stained that creamy face

With glaucous fanatic light—what was the charge
Her pouting lips seemed about to read?
Desertion? Slipping by your death? The man
Who died in your place being your poetic soul?
(You remembered the fright when you let Robinson fall.)
Would you be punished for that murder soon,
A coward expatriate in a living shell?
What judgment was due since you had cheated death?
You pondered the worst of pain, and then because
You had heard just enough of what the world
Was like above the Rio Grande, you knew
Your fate, updated from horrors that lurked before,
Seeking to dry your life out to a page:
Critics, poets, students and lecture halls,
Interviews, readings, traveling, expectant faces,
Faces of disappointment, shreds of sleep.
No doubt their stereos and air conditioning,
Televisions, politics and smog,
Jap automobiles, tenure, credit cards
Would keep you distracted while you endured it.
Until the roof falls in, they seemed to smile.

You thought of thirty years and what you did
Without thinking of what you did, just felt.
Was this *The porchlight coming on again*?
The world and not the page? What meant it all:
Some gun running for freedom-fighting clowns,
Getting shot at once while fleeing blind
For life under a palm-serrated moon,
A little marijuana smuggled north,
Aztec relics, blue snakes from Belize,

Even a parrot business—all for free,
Each for the cells' needles of self-content
Or what the turbid body thought was such?
What had you been in this kapok of your life—
Observant, compassionate, or a sponge of sense?
Why parchment-thin children, their noses oozing flies,
Dying old men lifting that rusty cross,
One raked drop of cocksblood on your cheek,
Mudfleas and swimming pools near vague saloons?
Were jaguars real or just on muralled walls?
Was the dysentery leeched out of your ass
By pity for the cracked fingernails
That picked the leached-out corn, for the strataed rot
Of blood-encurdled, lost Tenochtítlan
Whose influence, seeping up through modern life,
Was metaphor for all you thought we were?
Midnighted under San Francisco Bay,
Its waves above flat as Nebraska's heave,
What of the paintings, bebop, photography,
Movies, green wormwood of all pianos lost?
Poetry's ganglions still entwine their grip
On bridges and water, jungles, every mask.
Had you lived with them or become a character?
Her lush green eyes were linked by a chain:
They both descended, flowing about your wrists.

Gold crusted sun tarnishing the street,
The Mexicans stared, even the dull police,
At your thin shape among the gringo youth—
Your hands clasped before you—shuffling north
Toward all the steel, glass, plastic. Mouldering books

17

Will preserve you for us, won't they? *"Wondrous life!"*

The girl's slim legs rippled in the glare. . . .
You felt no irony. You desired none.

Hangover in Memory of James Wright

Clotted phlegm knots my throat.
Arid, spumy spit clouds from my mouth
like spider sacs.
My eyebrows have termites,
and I've never even been to Minnesota, James.
Your life wasn't wasted. If anybody
reads and loves this poem
mine won't be, either. My best friend
once said that most poems have
an ordered group of images and a patchwork philosophy
tacked on. My Coke gets flatter. Let them find
philosophy here.
You were lifted, at that instant, to
whatever novalike plane it was that caused
the water moccasin to carry those fish in its mouth
from their drying pond to its own, full and fresh;
that caused the giant sea turtle to keep that woman afloat
for three days. I sometimes
bite my tongue in my sleep.

For All Hostages

When the revolutionaries come,
burning my Wallace Stevens and Saint-Saëns,
will I regret I chased
women and men like a fleshy mist,
wanting to plunge in and suffocate
but rarely even feeling short of breath,
that I loved boyish girls and girlish boys,
loved whiskey almost more than either,
that I tempered drink and lust, so surviving
to stand there in the smoke and broken glass?

Will I have written those poems—so excellent
that they'll be burned as well,
remembering then that words are souls themselves,
they tune the eons of our hiving blood,
that no flung torch will spread such
teeming red,
that God is an impostor, not a star,
that love splits night's carapace,
revealing pulpy heaven.

In Memory of Ezra Pound

I sat smothered in traffic that morning
as the radio told me.
One day on a radio he had said
"You ought not to be in this war."

They noticed, I thought. Did I expect
tears to magnify the soggy day?
My voice said *oh*. It was like
someone trying to kill me over the telephone.

Suddenly I was carried
by a crowd of swart gondolas
stroking down narrow waterways
toward a gray east oil-rainbowed with the sun.

I floated then past barren Venetian sidestreets
like shifting fissures on a great pearl:
yellow garbage inlaid the black canals,
rose façades crumbled from marble stairs.
The air was glass-green. One could walk,
and I left the ebony vessels and came ashore,
lost in a maze of towers, doorways—then,

I turned a corner—a plaza, a pulsing crowd!
Hippies, cameras, red balloons, and there—
dark cape rippling, straight as a column, gaunt,
eagle hands and green beryl eyes,
face chiseled under the Russian hat

(the crowd fell away as the cameras whirred)—
what could one say? What,
if he saw Zeus, maybe, walking the earth in disguise?

I found myself ascending, by elevator,
with contemporaries. I thought of this line:
"Not to have lived, but to have taken place."

For Yukio Mishima

Not that you died—
not that the steel,
sharpest that moment in all its 300 years,
serrated your corded tendons so slowly;
not that your entrails slimed out
like answers to some question of life
veiled in your meridian's indigo;
not that Morita slashed your neck so clumsily,
or even that the photograph of your head
was published around the world,
but that the guardsmen in the parking lot
laughed, and cursed your self-knowledge—
a porphyry-veined commitment to that penultimate
quivering horizon before explosion of orange-blood sun.

But that laughter was too much a part of
the concrete, Coke bottles, and gas masks
to delay you. It was not
what sent you arrowing above transistors and whale
slaughter,
a thin steel of soul, invisible,
we seeing only its contrail,
rising to rake the sun's guts,
plunging back to the fleshed garden—
waterfalls, fruits, vines, purple wisteria death.

Death of the Bat-Poet

Cars pass down the night—their eyes are glass
and seem to diffuse a visible, liquorous whorl.
He sees an orange moon powdering in the clouds,
and slants of white as woodmist demons the road.
He has found forever now that *life*—that's all—
was what he set in lines—though he can still
feel the moon's fire pare the wind to voices,
swirl in the lean mist, or sting upward
through veins of grass.
He walks the highway's edge—bright swishing shapes!
Their speed and ebriate brilliance merge to say
You must know now that humans create alone:
All images, when touched, are only life.

Though far dawn will tarnish the mist,
trees cannot walk in wind—they only hiss.
Clouds make in the moon's powder
a closing fire that draws him in too deep:
in a world of moon and eyes
the headlights pierce to coned sleep.

Once

Once, in 1949,
in Eastabuchie, Mississippi,
while my fingers were rooting
a gritty carrot from the earth,
there was a blast, a roar
louder than that first helicopter
I had seen a month before.
I wasn't there to see the flash
of red and black in the tall magnolia,
or hear the spang of feathers
on the tin roof of the garage.
All I did was run to the yard
and discover, nestled in my grandfather's hands,
an ivory-billed woodpecker, dead,
punched through with shotgun pellets,
a thick gout of blood on its beak,
blood bright as its head or a magnolia seed.
The rarest creature of earth,
and I saw one, fallen to earth,
but less precious to me than the helicopter
which had sliced and dipped so silverly.
"I wanted you to see it," he said.

Jean Sibelius Bags a Soviet Plane, 1948

The maestro's yard, near mossed, penumbral pines,
Echoes the bluesteel hunting rifle's crack:
The fighter circles, wings off—was it a Yak
9 or Mig 3? No matter. Another shines
In cloudsifted sun, dropping lower. He fires again,
Leading the target this time with a vow
To sacrifice his frozen *Eighth* if now
He pierces the smirking aircraft, causes pain
For one damned Russian cog . . . so slivery smoke
Trails from the engine. A wobble. The pilot turns
East, igniting oil billows out. *Fate's joke*,
He thinks, watching the smeared speck as it burns,
Roils brumy below horizon, its soundless crash
Too soon avenged by his music's snowclean ash.

Camera Obscura

We can still hear them cough,
in counterpoint,
when Furtwängler hushes Beethoven's thunder.
Later, crushed out in the bomb shelter,
they appear—faded, flat on the drizzling film:
arms that heiled nervously, perhaps,
or legs that swaggered high
jut from mounds of timber and brick,
rayed in the stillness following
another orchestration from the skies . . .
Deine Zauber binden wieder,
Was die Mode streng geteilt . . .

Smudged buildings, trees; we see them watch
a laced skater twirl under white skies.
They smile; eyes are dark as foxholes,
limbs lax as though
they had pushed their wheelchairs back
from the Russian front.

Uniformed boys in line:
a 12 year old receives the Iron Cross—
he might be my kid brother shaking hands
with a robot—men, guns—now he's gone—
back to the front? dying because of that one handshake . . .
gebrauchsmusik . . . snow filling his open, surprised mouth?
Or does he work now in the Volkswagen plant?

We see them in grays, blacks:
who will bear all our colors?

To Lorca

We will not find you
though the afternoon sleeps like Egyptian gold,
though feet may pause over your groin,
though the two moles on your cheek nourish that phlox
and the white snails of your eyes are melted by lime.

What you were is the thirst of an orange tree,
the fire of those ants in its roots.
What you are will always be whatever we seek.

Mal de Siècle (I)

Richtofen's eyes locked on eighty planes:
Eighty tarnished the earth with streaming dust—
His body, data flowing in its veins,
Printed crosshairs on his retinas.
But for all the strutted extensions of his bones,
A tall, black-silkened woman came to him
When he lay wounded—identity unknown
Yet faithfully apparent: was she a slim
Tissued elixir contacting his heart's red spark,
That creature condensing in every hero's sheen?
Or did she rise from the swarthy cross—stark
As death's footprint on his scarlet triplane, stung
From suffering, merely to vanish? Gasoline,
Dope, wine, blood, fire failed him. He died young.

Under Halley

It should have blazed above us, a fountain of peace,
or at least burned cold, wide like a frozen Danube
letting the barbarians cross—mere iron and ice:
how glorious then our cleansed blood or machines.
But Halley skulked by, belied our old photographs,
our aging encyclopedias, all those books
which lovingly prepared us for forty years
to be thrilled, terrified, and purged at once.
We feel cheated, disinherited,
but bear our disappointment, wouldn't go back
to the failing, spawning culture that viewed it last:

In 1910 the world wound down to war
as the fuzzy star foretold the lingering deaths
of Art Nouveau, icebergs of privilege—
and the music of an undead century
shrieked as it was heated to plasma and streamed.
Mahler's *Tenth* grew under Halley's frozen spall,
his heart erratic, wheezing, dumping its love
for the psychotropic, igneous bloods of earth,
for his faithless, veering wife—love in sounds
that cauterize forever like yellow sun
the fearblack nodule gelid in our hearts.
Just two or three more months of life was all
he needed, to orchestrate that nucleus.

Delius saw it, perhaps intoned its glow
behind his eyes as he surrendered his sperm

to the warmth of a Parisian prostitute
who passed him the coiling spirochetes in exchange,
his music of bodies breathing terrestrial hope
diminished by bodies orbiting through the blood
as coldly as the unflickering fire above.
His mind, receding outward to glazing dark,
jetted final, furious, opalescent flares.

Scriabin gazed on it, surely being inspired
to complete his last fiery poem, wherein
the besprent universe seared to a whole
and moved to music the comet's ellipsing showed.
The same phosphorous logic vectoring its return
hurried the germs from his lip to scald his brain:
O harmonic breaths of uncompleted touch!

Griffes observed it, chromaticized the blue
clear atmosphere into a peacock tail
in Xanadu, on which eyed comets swarmed
through a plumviolet fever, melting down
all breath into a liquid clot of lung:
his dream of antique star watchers would come.

Just one shot of penicillin would have saved
their lives, those grainy antibodies shaping
transsolar wars within—but these are whims
like fabulous music that Halley didn't inspire:
they all beheld it arcing like a note
of iridescent crystal sound, but all
anyone left is that stiff *Comet Rag*.

Which is better than cheap T-shirts. Still, at least
our color photographs show the gas tail's azure
spitting through the white millennial dust.

And now as it's departing we must ask
just one *what* would save us from ourselves
so we'll be here when it returns? Inoculations
of love and tolerance would do it, we know.
One shot, one microcosmic capsule, but
of *what*, what life-poisoning chemical
will kill that part of life that wants to die,
slough the barbarians through the melting ice,
and keep the rest for Halley seething closer
next time, like music, through a purer, cleaner sky?

Morte d'Oscar

Outside, the sun bloats downward,
thick, red—sick on the sick air.
Darkness coming again here in Paris,
weary, like me, of the world's cigarettes and absinthe:
thin trees begin to pencil the fog
as streetlamps weave their webs of graygreen light.
Parisian night, as usual, impossible—
conjured solely in English dreams.

This hotel seems conjured—incredibly enough,
No. 13 Rue des Beaux Arts. Within,
a second floor room—here under the white pile
of spread and sheets my swollen body is warm.
No colored phials gleam beside the bed
so my gaze is lost in veins of the leaded lampshade—
is it Mary's chrysolite eyes I seek in the glow
or the browntoned gardenia of the moon?

The scalloped mirror gawks; the mantelpiece shrugs obscenely
like one surmising Victoria's coming death.

That massive clock of bronze and swirled marble,
supported by a crouched lion,
seems wispy, delicate to my slanting eyes
as iridescent wrists of alien glass. I asked,
"Qu'importe le verre, pourvu qu'on ait l'ivresse?"
And will become beautiful, being utterly useless.

Gottschalk in Peru

Viva la Revolucíon! their screams
Through frenzied Lima: Gottschalk, caught in the street,
Dives to a mouldy cellar—curled up, he dreams
The ricochets above are indiscreet
Piano notes spalling a savage salon.
To think, Chopin, Berlioz once shook these hands
Shaking today near the source of the Amazon
And then, emerged, obeying hammered commands
To help drag bodies, lining them by rows
In a pharmacy courtyard. Soon he'll touch Brazil,
Where peritonitis, with its crescendos
Of ache, will orchestrate a stern quadrille . . .
But now, hands Liszt has envied ripple, splash
Through fountains, glissand a corpse's limp mustache.

Burton on Fernando Po

A sodden, mosquitoed lump in Africa's armpit:
Even their liquor was lousy—he brought his own,
Then sailed to Lagos for more; slimy like spit
The harbor there, so back to the island's stone-
Edged jungle he came, ambassador to flies.
In its dusty villa he could ruminate
On Nile's source, absent wife, how all speech dies
Through change, white lunar peaks. To masturbate
Seemed better than driveling pidgin Spanish—whores
Knew Arabic if he needed them. *Damned fool,
The Devil drives,* he wrote—those fevered shores
Of the continent's eastern side felt almost cool
In memory compared to idleness here:
Language his solace only—to impose it, sheer.

Keats in Hell

Sulphurous depths proved real, not just uncouth:
God was a monster after all. Goddamn.
Beauty was just the opposite of truth,
And Keats was still a virgin, thank you ma'am,
An unbeliever, sentenced thus to barf
His lungs eternally, just like back home.
That cap Fanny sewed, lined with her red scarf,
Transmuting now, scalded the cranial dome
With torrid iron . . . fever imploded, raged
Until his brain backfired on holy plots:
Its neurons fused to a neutron star which phaged
All agonies, and jetted forth not clots
Of mouthed blood but measured, violet sound
To purged for heaven, too quick for underground.

Adrenalin Night
(AD 406-966 BC)

Frozen Danube

Readers, whatever our fate, believe these words:
my name is Claudian, perhaps the last
true Roman poet, but whether I am or not
matters little—because my arteries
soon will be emptied, my poems left to you.

In the center of my eye was a glittering spike,
a rugged shard of Danube ice. I knew
the emperor's will had become that frozen spine,
contracted, prostrate, sheeting the river harsh
and solid—letting the Gothic hordes across.

A comet, one of those glazy flaring thorns
that stab the night increasingly, traversed
the sky in the eleven hundred and twenty-seventh
year of the City—what the Christians call
the year of their Lord three hundred seventy-four,
loosing in me an obsession with alien carts
and wagons grinding over bleak, unmoving waves.

The next year a vessel of choleric blood,
distended by anger to bursting, swamped all fires
seething through emperor Valentinian's brain
as he ranted at the Quadi. His coarse brother,
Valens, one eye gleaming a cataract—
the eastern emperor by his brother's trust—
permitted the first Goths to ferry the Danube
and settle within Imperial boundaries. This

was two years later, and though the warriors,
fleeing from Huns and other ravening filth
(the kind I shall not have to face, at least)
were forbidden to bring weapons, the usual careless
greed of Christian Romans allowed swapping
of clothes, carpets, daughters, and wives for the surly
honor of swords. Thus the Goths—themselves
Christian now, obeying that mercantile
meddling religion—abandoned Germanic respect
for women as free and almost equal members
of tribe and family; and they grudgingly knew
that Rome considered them vassals to everyone's master,
the triumphant Church—reinventor of the Soul.
(I think of the ashes settling from my wife's
funeral pyre—that woman who meant to me
what Rome's effulgence was—and breathe a prayer
to the all-feminine essence of this earth
that whatever immortal portion she shares with it
never learned to fear the gape of the Dogma God.)

At last, when the Gothic men were starved, reduced
to selling themselves as slaves for gritty bread,
they rose and struck their venal hosts. This ended
in the Battle of Hadrianople, where Valens, jealous
of his fellow emperor Gratian, sneered at accepting
reinforcements and met the tribes. He lost
two-thirds of his legionaries, and his life,
quietly burning in a farmhouse attic
after his bodyguard fled and the enemy,
not knowing he was inside, torched the roof.
His bones were never found. Imperium

will not recover: savage the army's pith
and its commanders. Even my own poems
praising our valiant general Stilicho
celebrate the triumphs of a Vandal,
and a Christian hypocrite at that—how easy
it was to lick his corpse-wading feet,
to plump his victories up for personal gain.

I regret supporting him, who even gave
his daughter to our sexless emperor's bed.
The champion of the West, he lets Alaric,
another would-be Roman general,
escape after each defeat. I see his game,
playing those Visigoths against the East
while always scheming to be called the savior
of both empires, uniting them under his son.
Yet this is the man who seems our only hope.
The day he falls, I know the certain scourge
of everything that matters to civilized
persons is imminent. Barbarians,
our new Christians (and so more full of pride
but no less of rapacity), will attack
Rome to glut their avarice, though perhaps
leaving the temples of the Nazarene
untouched, thus proclaiming their piety.
Comets and galling winter stars, *sidere*
flagrante brumali, weighed down as if I had toppled
through cracking blocks and sunk to the river's core.

Watching those frog-egg spots that swim upon
my eyes when I stare at the far cerulean ether,

I thought of my wife's convulsions, and of Rome's.
If the beggarly Jew had such strength to bind
this City with his death-adoring charm,
surely our gods still had power to save
themselves from extermination—that must be
what lack of worshipers is. Was it too late
for us to help their genius survive?

A man who had been priest of Mercury
before selling out to the desert god
had told me several years ago of rites
praising the Magna Mater, carried out
secretly underground—and in catacombs
that once sheltered Christians from the scorn
of Roman law and ancient mysteries.
It was west of the City, beyond the Field of Mars,
disturbingly close to the Church of Constantine.
In a slaves' cemetery under a tiny hill
an old tomb, dug out and fitted with steps,
led to darkness beneath the furzy mound.
I scouted the surface by daylight and then, armed
with a dagger under my cloak and four slaves
around me, faced the arid maze of tunnels
near midnight with a single torch in hand.
Frightened then, I was careful to have one slave
strew a trail of bright pebbles behind.

Moving through the stinking burrowed black
lit everywhere with white, tottering piles
of ratpicked skulls, some grinning with the pride
of martyrdom, we came to a sudden halt—

a wall of gravelly travertine blocked our way.
Here I prayed aloud to the Great Mother,
hoping someone would hear and come to show
a secret entrance to Her inner shrine—
if such a thing existed. Nothing. I raised
my voice, screamed in that porous, dusted dark. . . .

Days later I realized one must come alone
to this sanctuary, and bring an offering—
dejection had made me forget these simple things,
fear of Goths outstripping fear of gods,
and even of utter resignation. Next time,
I waited until the moon's invisible
first phase quickened the Goddess' power, then entered
the catacombs again, weaponless,
wearing a brown tunic, my only light
a greasy candle, but carrying safe inside
a leather bag two gifts to Cybele—
or rather one for whatever decadent priests
I expected to find (some gold), another for
Herself, whose words, I thought, if any came,
would be written with the ink of the new moon.

Among the presents Stilicho had given me,
a pagan, for my too-abundant acclaim,
was a crude idol his family had kept
in memory of their primitive northern home.
It was carved from a meteorite, tiny crystals
sparking its grayish-brown, and in the shape
of a pregnant woman with bloated breasts (whose large
vaginal niche was part of the very stone,

not the poor sculpting)—a boreal deity
probably worshiped or at least carried for luck
by sullen Vandals. The Great Mother's form
was unmistakable, and since it came
from fiery celestial stone, I thought it might,
returned to a tended sacred place, invoke
Her anger, if nothing else, against the haughty
opportunists and their hell-feeding god.

That night I stumbled through the powdery holes
mumbling low whatever I could remember
of Cybele's attributes; I chanted Catullus,
recited formulas meant to drag a woman
by her genitals to love me and be my slave.
As I neared the blockage, suddenly unctuous wax
burned my fingers, and then the candle flame
was eaten by its own smoke. I tried to imagine
the sobering dark as Her divine protection,
but failed, and panic began to brew its vomit
when stones scritched behind me and I yelped,
turning into the glow of a quivering torch—
laughing, snorting, with fright and relief. Revealed
by a smoky square of light, a dry coffin
had moved aside from its slant against the wall.
My eyes teared with dazzlement, and fearing
the darkness would return I scuffed madly
toward the luminous haze and found two spindly priests.

They were bald, robed in black, their faces pinched,
and whether they were eunuchs as of old
was uncertain. I tried to explain myself

but one motioned for silence; the other reached
for my gifts, which I surrendered. Then they placed
the offerings in a crumbling wall-recess,
signaled me to remove my sandals and follow
through an arched tunnel leading down and down.
They grinned as we passed far away from the light
but their eyes were flat, vacuous, opaque,
and I realized the torch had vanished—they carried
pitiful tapers, flickering as we sank
till the glistening rim of a final gulf appeared
and my bare feet suddenly felt the glacial stone.

One priest dragged a rope out of the dark,
passed it under my arms and around my chest.
I asked if the chasm below was the Mother's dwelling—
they nodded, tied the rope behind my back.
Sitting down stiff on the slippery verge, I twisted
to be quite sure the line was secured snug
around a rock as well as their waists—then trembling,
I shifted down into what was surely death
or Cocytus itself. It seemed that no time passed
until I sensed the bottom, becoming afraid
more of my strange presumption in coming to speak
for Rome and the masks of countless ancestral dead
than of being buried alive in this monstrous pit.

When my feet touched a polished floor, I saw
vividly with nerves—in absolute dark,
real as my skin, a terrace was around me,
plush leaves flanging over bricks, while stars
flawed between branches. Slowly, just as one knows

that the Milky Way moves, only magnified, I felt
vast breathing, then Her presence, firm as night.
A sexual thrill, rising from my stomach,
veered to a tart nausea in the throat
and hissed out of my mouth. Was this Her sign?
She was right there, steaming, invisible,
pure bodiless flux no mortal could behold,
but I finally saw a growing orange spark:
an amber jewel gleamed before me, moved
as if upon Her breast. In its depths, encased
eternally, a dead insect—no, a woman,
fly-black, naked, with closed eyes but alive:
held there in a squatting, foetal position,
she seemed to breathe in time with the heaving gem.
I thought that above her glow immense eyes
of liquid tourmaline gazed through my jolting heart—
if this dark woman imprisoned in stony sap
opened her lids, I would be certainly lost. . . .

I could no longer remember why I came.
It must have had to do with Her anger or pity,
with Rome, or else the Christians and the gods,
my beloved's coughing sobs and prayers for death;
wits were blank—I was now possessed by Woman:
a being not any mere mother of gods
and men—but earth's energy and enigma.
In this cave with night around like fluid stone
I was drowned in her essence—a universal seed,
a guiltless perpetual vortex drawing all
to dream of transcending sex, religion, or love—
the love men waste on words and women sell,

the love squandered on marble Rome, the love
Christians assign to every bestial pain—
obscenity compared to what Woman is:
the black, sucking mass of her anima,
a violet-edged orb that mutates blood.

Cybele's face hid too close—in terror I felt
fine languorous hairs quiver at edges of lips
and a fluence of mouth opening to exhale
excrescence of living clove, salivary nuance of heat
reaching, encroaching, ghostly cerements of touch
in the veined, resinous night . . . tresses or leaves
or an opiate breath swept my feet away, I fell
forever (the circling stone was grained like sky)
between tangible darks—mouth, voidblack hair—into
Her star-swallowing body—and I worshiped night
and loved a blindness of ganglions swiftly stripped
from penis, hands, and brain . . . I struggled to cry
this is what we will lose with Rome, but my voice
congealed, every tissue a torrent of ice.

Sometime later I came to myself and felt
the rope squeeze my ribs, lifting me out.
Choked, I fled the cave, empty of feeling
as the priests' eyes of light. So now I know
and you will understand, too, whenever you live,
that Stilicho is doomed and so is the woman
we thought was Rome but instead is earth's own life.

In a few days, dressed in my whitest bordered toga,
I will climb the Caelian hill, breathe cleaner air,

and standing far above Rome, look toward the tomb
where my wife's urn lies; settling under a tree
I will drink from City, river, and sky—then at sunset
(perhaps in a fading flare of vermilion and gold)
my dagger will glint like the Danube's jagged sheen.

Death of Caracalla

Caracalla died while taking a piss—
scarlet his long cloak, firewinged the eagles
goldwoven on its border, protecting him not.
Near Carrhae in the desert he stopped for relief
where palms slanted athwart a scythe of moon,
his back turned by a rock. Where urine foamed
the sand, steam arose, and in its mist
faces—the ghosts of Crassus and Geta—laughed:
though the emperor twisted and shrank, Martialis' blade
cleft under his ribs and burst the heart,
and he rolled in the cloak—only the blond head visible,
the high, leafstraight nose and sunbrown face
calm, almost smiling, as if he knew
his young successor Elagabalus
would squeal to the same fate in a toilet in Rome—
his body submerged in shit down the sewer's maw.

Marcus Aurelius at the Colosseum

The blue and yellow light of afternoon
Will dwindle into sameness. Swords and sand,
The flick of blood, dull helmets, thumb and hand,
All but endure until the rising moon.
Why do they look up with their tired demand?
The blade will fall, if not now, then too soon
For my aging eyes tomorrow. Even the wound
Cut in clouds by the rising sun is bland.
Some men say jewels and fluent bodies sting
As fierce in mind as in the tangible guts,
But red mouths pouring words into my ears
Have an old rhythm, like a sword's flat swing.
This cadenced sadness of the senses shuts
My skull, while another opens without tears.

Hadrian at Tivoli

I made this place to think, and wait for him.
Will our union come only when body cedes
These glades of ferny dark, night made to bring
Him here? The fountains gush, channeled, pushed by
Anio's pressure up through sand and rock—
Water pumps from massed tangles, pummels into
Air, and turns back on itself, electrumlike.
Showering splashes over green stone, coiled
Swirling rot of limbs and roots, slim weeds
That rustle like young steps. These cascades smoke
A cooling sound through darkness—shadowy sound
Never to burn out. They wash among trees
And paths, walks and statues—statues all
Of him . . . columned arches, curved stones spidering
Over pools.
        Here on this chiseled obelisk
He is stone, but was not so mortally static,
The lips not so pursed but moving always
For a laugh or kiss—a looseness. He was almost
Everything that moved, unlike this carven
Form—graceful, but not him. It is too dense,
As every pulsing fountain is not blood,
Wound traceries of reeds and pulp not veins,
Not flesh. Water is cold, thin—blood is soft,
Those lips were fluid palps with redolent breath,
Not tissue, thick, but moist sacs of lightness.
He was veritable flux, hair and skin,
Green eyes radiate from a myth of black.

More alive than water, he died in water—
A stillness brought him from the soily Nile.
At least I found him smooth—safe from
Crocodiles and their yellow mossed teeth.
Smooth he came—I found him. Like Osiris
He sprouted from the slime . . .

The Syrians say life separates him from me
But I feel him present—in the fountains his laugh,
Loins in their ejaculating spouts,
Soft sucking of the night sigh, jady smells . . .
The roses ache for redness—thorns are leaves, thorns
Are leaves . . . he is here—and far southeast, marbled
That city—his—they kneel to him, they know
He was . . . he is . . . enskyed . . . starred . . . a god.

Last Days of Juvenal

With Hadrian supreme he grows a beard at last:
No more the barber's stinging lotion reeks,
No more blood-strawberries fatten on his cheeks
To require daubing with an itchy plast.
O freedom of respect for his whitegray nap,
Face's rugosity hidden safely beneath
(Although it's true this curling, mossy sheath
Makes him look Greek, or worse, an oiled satrap
From Parthian stews). But comfort in his age
Outranks what deference his patrons show,
Whether more or less: he will no longer rage
At Rome as on some cracked column a crow
Might squawk hoarsely at depilated whores
Drifting, like him, toward Caesar's gilded doors.

Trajan at the Persian Gulf

Squatting here in sunset, having come
not to paradise but a barren beach
in Asia, I watch, far out, a sandstorm sweep
this sea—blindness scouring poisonous waves—
and celebrate no Alexander's triumph.
If I could discover a way to separate
usable water from this inlet's salt
that knowledge would outlive all my victories.

In Dacia I saw a bee preserved in amber;
at Petra, embalmed in honey, a dead child:
black hair swirled within gelatinous orange—
a small face clouded close with perfect teeth;
Alexander himself I viewed in Egypt: jeweled,
shrunken but youthful, sinewy, circumsealed
by a xanthic slab of resin shagged with gold.

Here there are lakes of naphtha, wells of gas,
shimmering asphaltum oozed in glazy pits:
since, if lighted, they burn for centuries,
might not these substances also conserve
the body, innumenize its flatulent pulp?
No will-o'-the-wisps, they lured me on this far,
consuming fires, yet like the body's need
for salt and water, near perpetual.

But there is no water for my legions here
in the River Tigris' crotch, where her freshness becomes

a saline marsh . . . and then an ocean with sandstorms.
Beyond lies India with its mildewing rains,
but those defeated Alexander too,
flaying his men to mutiny, him to lead them
rasping back through the empty Gedrosian hell
(torpid hundreds of miles yet to the east)
where sixty thousand perished. Probably
some Macedonian corpses flake there still,
humiliated, mummified by sun,
parchment lips intact around a hiss.
Is this the fate that I might bring on men
who gladly would immolate themselves for me
in this landscape of flammable soil and air?

My own death will be an immolation
on a column of fire brighter than any jets
combined of these fierce desert combustibles—
more splendid than this slow strata of gloom
as Asia's dark sloughs over the briny sun
leached in its violet transmarine desert gale.
I scorn to be a lingering husk. My pyre
should reach for stars as the body's blazing fumes
swirl to sear the clouds and later fall,
congealed, as cooling rain. What Trajan was
the most, his pitch and spit, will be dispersed
to ether; what the least, mere caustic ash,
hidden in stone. My conquests will be lost
like the young king's, but our sweat—fluid so like
this water simmering here—will color time.

Domitian in August

Here I sprawl, Domitian, the molting, earthy god
Painted ebon like my guests but with languid eyes:
In this dim chamber senators eat black pies
(Served by sooty boyslaves and stuffed with sod)
While funeral dirges tremor; chewing his clod
Each conscript father, relieved between his thighs
By the slaveyouth sucking out what quickly dries
(Juice, assurance), sees another dark servant plod
To place before him an urn, eponymous.
Why not? On September XVIII that autonomous
Ration of death will settle (it's foretold)
In me. *Fore*. One cannot escape the old
Truth, even with Minerva's owly scope
In marble mirrors. So Rome must be bald of hope.

Red Skeletons of Herculaneum

Yes, lady scientist who glues my shards
together with such ease, I was a slave:
those lesions in the bones of my upper arms
told you that, made when muscles shredded
(how I shrieked) that day I had to carry,
ten years old, my infirm father's load
of dead gray firewood, brittle as my red limbs
pitted from lack of calcium, as you see:
at twelve my skeleton shuddered as I was pressed
into soft ground by the humid, enshrouding skin
of older, sunfish-odored male slaves
using me thoughtlessly as my owners did—
but still engraving in me the pang of life—
till very soon the mistress took me in
to care for her daughter, that child you found in my arms:
downy yet shrill and never caring for me
she spit in my face once, but as we ran
from the waxy chalkflocked cloud I carried her,
panting hopeless cheer through her gritty hair,
to the beachfront chambers that became our tomb:
packed in choking dark with the mouldy brass
stench and taste of terror I covered her,
strained to soak that aura from her pores,
tried to shield her with my scrawny flesh
as the gases seethed our lungs to crackling husks
and the boiling sludge enveloped us with the sound
of vast black mothwings beating on the sun.

Agrippina

Inside the arena, bitchy in the moon
After the mob and emperor had gone,
A gladiator stumbling with her in the ring,
Agrippina tore her robe and threw
Herself down, naked, cried to the sweating man
To take her there in the hot stink of the blood
That wined his hands, blood of another, killed
For her, since she outscreamed all of the crowd.
That stroke on the red sand laved within her, red
Is joy's color, red palms intoxicate
The pores, red is a ferment of groins and thighs.
They coupled there in the arena's center—death
Dried on her from his clutches—jewels were grit,
Empire a bloated, redhaired son gone mad—
None of it mattered in this sandy knead
Of him and the spawn ablutions of her limbs,
The brining of tongue on tongue, sparks of pain
With sand in the labia and then his shuddering squeeze
As though her body were all unbroken grapes.
Seeing the moon above the emperor's box,
Feeling the rasping breath and the scoured back,
Spreading herself, forgetting all her power,
She might have cried *Strike the womb!* as she did
Later, just before the sword's last thrust.

Caesar in Parthia

Ctesiphon burning, low sun an amber date
Tumid through smokeblued palms, those eagles lost
At Carrhae recovered, he muses on the cost
So far, in this consecrate campaign of his fate:
Prepared with resin-hardened shields for the weight
Of Parthian arrowstorms, with a spring-slaked host
(Mirage-creating horsemen—doubtless the most
Ever trained to fool the eye or prove Rome great),
He triumphs, yet remembers how near he came
To Styx instead of Euphrates—this current fame
Would have bled, aborted, had not Servilia spied
On her wavering son Brutus, and then denied
Glory and martyrdom both, twisting his ear
And leading him to Caesar, calmer of fear.

Clodia

Love's ecstasies were never enough for her
And her black, drugged hair, body of supple chalk,
Grackle-sheening eyes: she craved design
More durable than flesh. Her Muse's mind
Drew menlike souls whose bodies she could stir
Almost into becoming men. Their talk
Tendered all the ambitions she would find.

Then he appeared, a poet who could bind
All plots and senses with the body's myrrh
And taunt her with a love that was a birth
Of elegies—so she twisted him and he died.
Despite those mindless, perspiring hours, to her
No passion was as fierce as when she lied.

His blood diffused like wine through the dark earth,
The Pomptine marshes dreamt malarial sleep,
She gazed on white columns with her great black eyes—
But the words of poems, like starlights, flickered steep.

Egyptian Love Poem

Supposing the belief that the souls of those killed by infectious plagues (the active wrath of the gods) could not enter the skyey realms of Heaven and the House of the Dead. Their bodies were salt-dipped, wrapped in linen, and buried in the desert without regard for social class.

I loved you, Nephthys, beside the slain Nile.
Your body then was soft papyrus
and your breath sweet oil.

Then fever came and passed like many leopards—
Egypt's green entrail was gnawed out.
Wealth could spare no one from the quick brine—
and your breath dropped down to one clear stop.

We carried you from your house in the crusted gauze,
my battle scarves lowered you into the sand.
For you the sky is barren—there was no need
to bury wine for a soul that could not rise.

The Nile is gorged now, Nephthys. Stalks are tight,
their piths spill over the lapped slime.
Jewels heighten our umber bodies, but you are out there—
I have come to pray that the soul can truly die.

Tanous

(At the MacArthur Museum, Little Rock)

My friend and I. A glass case. Within,
The small mummy of an Egyptian girl.
Her crust, wound tightly in a human shape,
Hides what priests once softly glazed within.
An X-ray, though, reveals the hollow skull
("The brains were drawn with wire out through the nostril")
And a black loop around the smudged wrist
Which can only be a bracelet—but slim hands
Snaked in gold must never stroke it now.

Other cases stand here. They contain
White scarabs, lapis gods, Eyes of Horus.
Men died for these, but this is Little Rock—
The stones are cracked, the scarabs steatite,
The lapis gray; yet all this is valued,
Hushed people come here yearly, though these objects,
Their age making them more than junk, all mock
Douglas MacArthur's birth here in this house.

The mummy again. Her name, *Tanous*,
Inked on the husking linen. We imagine her eyes,
Two blue stony fisheggs, sense her hands,
Now mudhard . . . did they once crush papyrus
And feel the foaming juice, green in the sun?
Did she once hold a living scarab? Maybe
She thought the beetle a noisome, spiny thing.
Then natron sucked her mouth. She holds her tongue

64

Quiet, unfoolish. Surely cats were killed,
So many, to lie with her. Here we are.

Why do we love her, dead? Because she will
Endure virginity throughout all time, like art?
Ourselves, our wives, that guard who eyes us so
Peculiarly—we are all muscle, fluid, hair:
But we would kiss, hold *Tanous*, taste of her
Before we worshiped MacArthur's rotting flags . . .
Were humans ever meant to love dead wars?
She never reached our age; our bones will not
Hold shape three thousand years. I touch his arm.

Modern Poet and Calypso

An island ringed with boulders—huge sea-grapes
Rising and crumbling gradually into soil.
Grass billows backward from the cliff—
The deep, rimy grass, flowing through vineyards
Where wet lattices stab among the leaves:
Long ago, poets rested here.

Lamps streak those garnet-terraced chambers
Where man and goddess sleep. Tonight she lies with him
Because he strained ashore, knowing his right
To ease down in ancient gossamer
And wash through her divinity like sea foam . . .
(To come here, some have written of languid oars
And surf, poppies, burgeoning island streams;
Others of the burning fog of cities,
A few of all the sorrow children bring.)
He wakes suddenly—arms heavy with her—
That body's tangible light enphialed in his stare—
And thinks of ships: he listens to a nymph's waved song.

She welcomed him. But now he has drunk
From the moving, porous vessel of her mouth.
These last hours murmur awhile, and soon
The gauze of night will ravel—his stay will end.
Fire and clover. Aching into her
He stalls the dawn and every new care
Though he cannot create here; his is no seed
She can generate—the others found this out.

The shore remains, though mariners are few,
But this is not earth—his thoughts are earth . . .
Islands still lie unsummoned . . .

>Nymphs sing thin:
>sea brings the dawn through arbor
>in mists of bees—
>melting, the sunrise like gasoline.

II

Adrenalin Light

Beginning

Thought-dolmens ranged behind a silver beach
where the omnilingual sea transpires with ease:
I visit there by heart each day
when other men's dark grains become my own.
There in the blood's vital waste of time
I breathe to think of the ribbed insouciance of leaves,
of the faience hues in our cleanest skies,
of—why not?—shaggy plowrows
fronting this sea whose salt will spice, not sterilize,
the must of the earth.

Moorish Idol

Like fleshtrailed moon, the idol of the Moor,
Yellow-phosphored as the Kohinoor,
Seen submarine, might slowly undulate
While angling through an oceanic substrate
Among the grainy frequencies of light.
Surrounded, though, by glass, as if to spite
Our lust for uncleared mysteries, it dies
At the first touch of tainted water, plies
Belly upwards if bubbles cease a minute.
Snaring this creature in a Bengalese net
Requires brief ritual while it's released
(Amid shrill chanting, prayers for the deceased),
Quick with mystic absolving, back to creased
Seasurface in honor of its sheen of luck.
Zanclus cornutus: the fisherman has struck
Canary yellow, white, black gold at once
But must return it to the fluid, which blunts
His livelihood though not the fish's shape—
Sickled, horned; tradition on his nape
Demands it, serious as gasping gills.
Freed, the Idol streaks below to rills
Of coral searching for its mate. Its beak,
Scissorlike, snips the growth, rejects the freak
Intrusion of the breathless realms above—
That senseless glare where blurred shapes flail and shove.
Eventually its consort comes—their snouts
Touch once; then, tails together, green redoubts
Of living mineral veined with wriggly food

Lie open, fanned in sunlight's saffron brood
Of motes, starred fragments, phototropic veils
Where plankton navigate the warping sails
Of current. Human curiosity
Or hunger hauls them glossing from the sea
Only to have them die or win reprieve
Through vanity or superstition . . . believe,
Some do, but striped smooth scales, vertical fins
Trailing like moonflesh, each eye a black lens—
All these refute desire to encase
In transparent walls or fantasies, so faced
With life which suffocates in penned despair
Or blesses all that yowling in the air,
They reject both parching fluxes of emotion
Which lack the rationality of ocean.

Near Eastabuchie, Mississippi

I

This pond. A gray, manmade cup
sunk in a field surrounded
by pines. That child, we know,
fell from the bitterweed edge,
floated that day, threshed, and sank
as if flying; he looked up, certainly,
and saw his cries become silver globes
as the sky was whirled and sucked
into flawed milkglass—a dense
congealment of light, water, breath.

None of us ever knew this child
except as his drowning relates
to our own curdled vision of death;
we can even think of him as recalled
to some prenatal world of dream . . .
say he faded, painless, insane
with the pressuring quiet—a syrup
of pine-close, cricketless green—
the turgid center of our eye.
But what would all of that mean?

II

Now we walk toward the trees. Near the path,
the old Gunn place slants through the weeds:

A gnarled, gray house shows its ribs
as its builders might, lying in the earth.
Split shingles invite the thick moss
to thread the roof over, the porch
has crumpled into the field,
kudzu snarls round the outhouse.
Should we care what this ruin held?

The Gunns. No faces. They were born here
and too quickly we can categorize
their lives: how they axed out the trees,
saw the gravel roads mire, and the cows
swell with their calves and disease,
watched the *Grapette* and *Clabber Girl* signs
flake in the heat and lean.
We admit that the sky they breathed
was blue, clean, smelling like earth
in the Genesis they read and believed—
but some of us probably will think
of plowing-sweat, green bitter milk,
Mason jar whiskey and knives,
or a black man, naked and tied,
being hanged from a tall, scaly pine.
Our child, that unscaly thing,
slid out—but the Gunns, who lived here,
had seen 78 years worth of something
he avoided; and we, in our way,
think we have too—could their death
have been fluid, then? What was it like?
A collage of this house, briars, and sweat
in a black scripture of pine needles and dung?

What would you say of it? Like the door
of the outhouse meshed over with kudzu,
you inside, your stinks feeding the green?

Soliloquy Against McLuhan

The moon is still not gray to us.
Here we see it's like an eye, a slice,
A yellow attrition of ellipsing light.

Once it was thought dead souls went to the dark part.

No life at all. Nothing. Yes.
We do see ourselves on the moon, though.
It is not one hard stone; we now understand
That we have gouged phases, and often change
With ancient forces also: blue spheres,
A green fibrousness of flowing plants,
Seas, brows, wet hair: threadings we pile up
In an architecture toward that clear new moon death.

These skies, the moon, will outlast flesh. No doubt.
Some know that what flesh is is not yet known. Everyone
Makes what he sees out of himself. Herself.
Volcanoes are like us. We are not like them.
The earth has soft black veins. All veins burn.
A wraithing of shadows lids out the sulphur moon.
Flesh hopes that flesh hopes for more than flesh.

Earth

My skin continues when her skin begins.
As blind men see in dreams I feel her touch.
When the riotous breathing comes the body ends.

The dream is first an act: our flesh descends
Through separate discipline till the balance is such
My skin continues when her skin begins.

Touch is sudden as pain when body blends
A blindness of nerves into a piercing clutch.
When the riotous breathing comes the body ends.

Hair spirals on hair, pores valve, each surface sends
Its own genius into the unctuous rush:
My skin continues when her skin begins.

The cleaving and flattening peak—tissue expends
Our blindness out of itself it learns so much.
When the riotous breathing comes the body ends.

We seem green, fervorous sleep. A dream contends
That spasming, salty gods lie in a hutch.
Our skin continues when their skin begins:
When their riotous breathing comes our body ends.

Cavafy Poem

Because of our telephone conversation
you are coming at four o'clock
to see my kitchen of tricolored glass.

I have not told you
that my eyes are as green as that Cretan stone
dredged up by a Greek fisherman in 1908,
said to be from the stars . . .

and that I have no kitchen.

January 1

I drew breath through your hair
I whispered half in fear
"I love you" and you said
"And we love you" properly
Including your husband but
I held you for that swath
Of time exhaling slowly
The glory I'd drawn in
From just above your ear

Blues Poem

Tonight our friends play torrential blues
in this upstairs club—knowing you'll join them later
and sing to us all in that vibrant, drowning voice.
But now I pretend your song will be for me,
and we both relax, listen . . . for once you're sitting
next to me, with no one else so close
they can steal, hold your attention: the hairs on my arm
send out electrical leaders to attract
your flesh's lightning . . . in this musical blaze
we have to lean close, yell in each other's ears—
it's heaven: you look at *me* when you speak, our mouths,
our noses millimeters apart; your smile,
earth's most infectious, those clear, sibilant teeth,
your fine, newly-cut hair falling around
pure gold Chinese earrings—what else can I do
but beam my lipclosed grin in stupid joy.
Your husband, I learn, has said you can smoke and drink
tonight—a reward for combined efforts the last
three months—both of you sweet-breathed and sober. I watch
close as you light the first filtered Camel
in almost ninety days—not violently deep,
that first drag, no eyesqueezed, shuddered delight
twists your face: the action's still a habit,
that white pouring thick from your nose and mouth
easily blends with vaporous memories. Now
the smoke blows my way: for the first time
I breathe it greedily, hissing—it's *your* smoke,
has been inside you, in all the pink, foamy

infinite sacs of your lungs (which were just beginning
to lose the residue, the tincture and taint
of black tobacco pollution; your recurring cough—
our bane and worry—was disappearing). You claim
to sing better after a few cigarettes:
doubtless it's true—you gulp Budweiser as though
it is, and so I pray you'll get just drunk
enough to lean closer, and touch me more
than ordinarily, more. The guitar flares,
brilliant: you laugh, happy, I'm happy—a spray
of saliva flits from your mouth to my upper lip,
I lick it, ecstatic—joy of the blood of stars
exploding inside my head, my mouth aching
for yours . . . and I know the smoke will clot
until my eyes blister, but some is *your* smoke,
has touched your blood, and I breathe insatiably,
damning my health and yours for this short bliss.

Too soon your film instructor plonks his ass
down across the table, and so ensues
a lengthy, shouted conversation I still
can't hear—though in a fit of wounded pride
I scour my brain for several clever lines
to scream into your lush, gold-burdened ear
and make you turn and look at me and laugh,
noticing my existence off and on
until it's time for you to sing—and then,
eyes watering from the haze, I gladly share
you with the audience, because on stage,
incandescent with your perfectly human beauty,
you're so much yourself we don't know who you are.

Suicide Poem

And finally it comes down to the same tired scenario
you thought of years before:
the Mauser rifle (Spain, 1953), the World War Two
German ammunition with more lead than allowed
in the "rules of war"; a secluded backyard glade
open to the plain blue sky.
You'll not push the trigger
with your toe like Mr. Whatshisname in *Noon Wine*,
or that Japanese soldier in a photograph. No,
it'll be more *il faut mourir*: you'll sit down,
surely, bite hard on the barrel before you press
harder with your thumb. What else? Yes, that face,
called up from forbidden poems, what you injured
without meaning to, what hurts so much to love,
the last thing, her evanescent face.

To Her Husband

The only kid I hated enough
to bring down with a flying tackle
was one of your brothers, the one just older
than you—I won't say his name. This
was about the time Ray Nicholson said
to Gerald Nuckols on the muddy playground
"Boy, you look more like a raped ape
than anything I ever saw." They fought.
Maybe you were across the schoolyard then:
no one thought you'd ever grow
taller than me, six balding feet,
that you'd be a brave helicopter pilot
in the fucking war's last days,
spewing fire on their raped apes,
lifting our raped apes to musty,
laboring hospitals. No one dreamed
you'd marry a woman I'd later think
I couldn't breathe without, her blaze
making me the kind of man
doing apely things to feed that heat
as clean as the hate when I gasped forward
and tackled your brother from behind,
perfectly airborne, horizontal
when I struck hard, slammed him flat
on the dirty grass, never feeling
a damned thing except that ravishing
flare that lit up every vein.

Mal de Siècle (II)

Don't suffer now—the electric, sad proteins
You stirred inside were just beyond her means:
She praised Gauguin's paintings, but his green eye
Wasn't an image of yours. The vivid dye
So tincturing her wits was sensual,
She agreed at once, but the eventual
Glazing of satiation didn't remind
Her of your lovemaking—or that anodyned
Yet hazythistled lassitude which came
After each nacreous spasm. Never the same
Were any of those ardor-anointed days
Soaking your bodies in the oils light plays.
Don't suffer now—that aura's gone from you:
Prismatic love is what she can't pursue.

Withdrawal

Dead night. Night of inked stars. Night of your brain's
black fungus become anthracite. Night of each cell shaking
under your nails, retinas quivering like every drop of
silence saying *You did this. You.* Heartflinching night, each
spasm less real than bloodclouding presences of shame,
self-contempt, honest old despair. Do poems do this? Night
of the buried sky. Night past the point of return.

Dream of Krakatoa

And how would it be? 10:02 AM, realizing
bamboo, iridescent now,
is only giant, trembling grass.
Copper quiet like nothing ever felt:
cockatoos flap for life, salmon crests yawning
in a blaze of pinkwhite powder sifting;
breathing of earth, all islands become
your stomach,
quavering, a dream of vomit of earth's black wine;
low slate overhead, sea only
naked sand, fish flopping, gasping
like the cockatoos,
sky now merged with endless wall
of swift bile green . . .
Run, and run—and then
the sound, the sound they heard
in Texas,
adrenalin liquor spurting, breathscrape—
feet cut stones nails hair eyes . . . you.

Villanelle for the Greenhouse Effect

"Once it starts it's self-perpetuating—
A glassy, invisible screen forms overhead."
"Oh, yes. Well, you see, they're still debating."

"When the bloating, jaundiced sun starts saturating
The polar cap, the ocean shores will spread.
Once it starts it's self-perpetuating.

"We haven't even got the time for hating
These fools—whose thumbs won't twiddle when they're dead."
"All I can tell you is that they're debating."

"Then make them hurry up! We can't be waiting
For the screams and all the drowning that's ahead.
Once death starts it's self-perpetuating."

"Don't you think you're slightly exaggerating
This business? We've got twenty years, they've said.
After all, they aren't yet through debating.

"You must get some thrill from aggravating
Men in offices—what books have you read?
Regardless of your self-perpetuating,
You'll have to cool your heels, friend. They're debating."

New Moon

This moon could be a clipped fingernail
or a curve of burning tallow, and he walks
among the soft branches and tufts of weed,
feeling inside him a sliver of something stir
and set his teeth sharply, and flex his toes.

It is not fear he thinks of—he has left
the town quite willingly. The growing phase
that makes him tremble now is a power of sense:
the slit of moon bays in his retinas,
the darkness glows, his nostrils blaze with scent.

And the moon is young, so now he also knows
more blackness will be sliced away each night.
He wants to see her burn camphorously,
to hear voices needle on the wind,
and panting, hunt the fleeing spoor of veins,
but doubt harangues this loping from deep craters
and cries for daylight and its rigid trees.
What will he be when she is full and gouged?

He crouches to watch that lean but bright promise
of curling toes and nails, the lengthened teeth,
the harsh fur easing from his pores, the surge
in struggling flesh of brute adrenalin light—
all nerves, it seems, will dilate to release
bonewhite vibrancy from his aching throat.

But if he utters the full moon's dissonance
and feels the dark become a living thing,
will pure awareness end in naked sun
with grass smelling as if it lacks green,
or will an animal hide like a fallen god?

Already leaves are vaporous; bushes wake
with rustlings; now his eyes can touch the heat
of bark and water, rocks—the life of earth,
that force living outside of any dream . . .
Mist draws over the trees as the thin moon
slumps through a jaundiced hazing toward the dawn.

Algolagnia

Tonight I learned to half-vomit
and still light and smoke
that cigar; decreed
the squamous tingle in my side
not to be cancer;
felt the hardened miasma of my T-shirt armpit.
I was reconciled to gravity, and
a haunch of moon sat on an oak limb.
Three stars needled.
Truth: bitter diamond.

Sentry

I'm the one who always dies at night for you
In all the movies, novels—even life:
Somehow the night knows but it never tells—
Knows I'm going to die yet doesn't smirk
Or shudder in a warning jest before
The cord seethes around my throat, before
The hand crimps my scream and blackened steel
Sleeks between ribs, before the rifle butt
Stamps a spiderweb throughout my brain.
I'm legion, and each time you see me die
Failing in my duty, though I kept
A decent watch, usually, but then
Always, I nod or droop to sleep at last,
Or jerk toward that skittering in the brush
Where the hero's thrown a rock—and then it comes.
Did you ever think what my nights are like—
Knowing they're out there and no matter what
I do they'll still skulk up behind my back,
Strangling, stabbing, bashing. Hero-fodder,
That's what I am, and also don't forget
It's no fair fight—your brave warrior's only
A sneaking coward—though his mission's just.
How boring to be a necessary death!
I pray for a quick and painless bludgeoning
But anybody can swing a club; therefore,
The blade's keen scorching or the hissing cord—
Both showing off the hero's strength and skill—
Are used most often in my sacrifice

To the gods of convenience and cliché.
Perhaps I love this earth . . . I could whine
That I adore my mother and girlfriend too,
But that's no help—you won't ever stop
Heart-racing toward my death. Is it because
You almost never have to see my face?
No. I'm here because like all of us
No matter where I turn I turn my back.

Memory

Window screen: moths whirr against the light.
The moon broods in webs of mould. Night seeps.
Those companions, those sweating humans we loved,
seem like cracked mummies in ancient wax.
Time flaws, displaced like water by memory's black stone,
and our saps flow, resinous; love of old wounds is resinous
like those syrups that occluded the mummies' eyes.
Lost sighs stalk as if wrapped in linen.
When you had a broken leg you walked
like that. Forget.

In Lieu of the Truth

Metastasis occurs in rhetoric
and also when a writer's lung cancer
sops along the lymph up to his brain.
My former lover (her thick, bituminous hair,
sparking silver, still constricts my chest)
told me what her long-divorced friend said,
the one who doesn't like sex anymore:
"All the men will die first anyway—
you'll be left with only women in the end."
My stomach twisted. "That's why I'm nine years
younger than you," I said, as if we shared
more than occasional hugs. "She must be sick."
This forces thought of another caring friend,
the lean, frizzy, laboring poet who can't
understand why I won't make love with her.
I want her fitfully but bitterly,
and exchanging the charmed saliva and oils of sex
would be an honor and a privilege,
but she has done what I have only wished:
had so much drenching joy of other lives
and the plasmic bodies that inhabit them,
that dread of an infection stronger than love
is more than lust and courage both can bear.
How, though, to say that to someone you adore?
Maybe my older love's wry confidante
never liked sex at all, perhaps those two
will spend blank last years as their mothers did
with tired daughters wiping their crepey butts

in rest homes; maybe my skilled, sinistral friend
(her lower lip, curling out when we kiss,
almost makes me despise my own erection)
will understand and even forgive in time
if she sees that most of our scarring loves,
our humiliating, boneweary decencies,
and even that terrifying basic need
for each other's touch can suffer metastasis—
killer of writers but not their imagined worlds.
And so this poetry in lieu of the truth.

Canto

in memory of Ben Kimpel

If only all our paternal grandfathers
were one-eyed Russian Jews—
who belched white guncotton nights
in Dostoevski's face, slobbered nobly drunk and married
on the steppes' acid wind,
who swam scratched but safe through
the strawberry jam mud in the pogrom's veins.

Seas of mud viscous as puréed flesh;
lehars of mud cracked and dry as ancient violins;
ramps of love built of futile bodies
laid up the side of time's desert fortress;
the humid, porous moles of deferred desire;
the long, sculpted septum of deathscorning pleasure,
all these we would understand.

Kochab's bleared orange would cease to mock us,
innumerable Turkish cigarettes faze us not;
easily we could walk through vinegared alleys
of guttural language, read caves of books
uncomplainingly; tall, skinny girls with chocolate eyes
and hair like ringleted night might beckon us
at last, love us; one deep squint would prove
every human contempt dearer than starfaring aliens:
our blood could sing this to being, if only all
our fathers were one half one-eyed Russian Jews.

For Jessica S.

They say your mother danced for Hitler once,
then caught the last Dutch steamer out:
I see her running now (small, lean but hard
dancer's muscles runneling skin
which the murderer doubtless admired—*so*—as she leapt),
achieving the gangplank dextrously as it rose
to liberty and her fate of meeting and loving
in bombless countryside the war-
and booze-maddened Mississippi boy
who courted poetry in vengeful Paris. He was destined
to combine uniquely our Southern
with British imagery and speech,
to fail at last at living,
but not before her, who alone leavened his sad
fear, then took her bow, gauntly mapped
with those dark veins Dylan Thomas praised.
And he (who had met the glorious, sotty bard)
wrote three strong books, lectured, and unwittingly
scarred you with too much loving while often thralled
to bourbon, Salems, or handrolled weeds and old
Baptist hangovers climbing high on fire
spewn from your grandparents, one of whom had known
General William Booth, awaiting you all in heaven.
You, bewildered in English reconstruction
and stateside versions of slick prosperity,
heard a father's bent rage strumming your guts
to beats of a harrowing drum which combined
Beatles' racket and Dad's smoky breath

into richer throbs—and so took the sticks
to flee his talent, and your own.
You finally escaped him by becoming yourself
in a penisless pounding of *this is what I am*,
a poem-flinging drummer—affirming beats
lounging above sleek, pedal-rhythming legs
between which lies that channel out of your heart.
I, a poet your father taught without
crushing my balls with affection or snuffling guilt,
say this: he knew (erasing Hitler's leers
at your mother's grace) the ultimate crush was love.

Honey

The clear, amber honey
flows from the jar . . .
we smear it on biscuits,
through the cells of toast.
In it some see trays of bees,
their close swarming like
bunched berries.
Some feel intensities of humming,
the striped solitude of drones,
      yellow vaults in darkness:
        hexameters.

Pavane for a Dead Princess

Day implodes into one sunset,
Then the mouth of night's spored kissing
Opens wide. Her chills have stopped.
Silks are weighty with her dark pressing.

Clarinets are mildly fueling
Palace air with myrrhlike burning.
Calmly grieving, the Emperor sees
Fuzzy stars crawl out like vermin.

Near the end he saw her bloating
Out of herself like a red star.
With the chills she novaed. Body
Flung out through light silk, nebular.

Now she gleams small and white. Hermetic
Walls protect her from earth's violence,
While her energy and meaning
Scatter out and out through silence.

Mal de Siècle (III)

Now even the old are afraid of dying young:
They too sometimes pause before making love.
Viral African monkey blood has sprung
Gibbering through our brains. Air heating above,
Plaguey in sun's unfiltered exhaust, sweats out
Few terrors concerning a winter born under smoke.
Contrary statistics only inflame the drought
Called apathy; our dreams try vainly to soak
Purulent dunes silting the rivers of sleep.
Now even the young are afraid of dying old
And seeing in fear to love a final result:
The world become gehenna or boreal cold.
Are psychic or bodily chemistries what keep
Making self-preservation so difficult?

When I Die

When I die let everyone love the shards of starlight,
let clear frost make a dazzling fish of earth;

When I die let multitudes read my pages,
let someone say my words were buffed chalcedony;

When I die let scientists build an inertialess drive,
let a bright ship leave for Sirius;

When I die let nations dress in green and orange,
let them know these were my favorite colors;

When I die let all read verses, love women, eat cantaloupes,
let some dream of carved glass, some of the proud lips of Hadrian;

When I die let many shout my name all day,
let them know that by then Villon may have told me everything.

Notes on the Poems

The Capture of Weldon Kees: Weldon Kees (1914-1955?), American poet who spoke before his disappearance of suicide and of going to Mexico and living under an assumed name. His car was found at the entrance to the Golden Gate Bridge. He was a jazz musician, painter, and filmmaker. "Robinson" is a recurring character in his poems.

For Yukio Mishima: Yukio Mishima (1925-1970), Japanese novelist who committed *seppuku* (ritual suicide) at the Japanese Self-Defense Forces headquarters on November 25, 1970, after failing to incite the soldiers to rise up and restore the emperor as *de facto* leader of Japan.

Camera Obscura: The Germans words, from Schiller's "Ode to Joy," appear in Beethoven's Ninth Symphony and mean "By your magic is united / What stern custom parted wide." *Gebrauchsmusik* is "music for use," a modern term.

Under Halley: Gustav Mahler (1860-1911), Austrian composer; Frederick Delius (1862-1934), English composer; Alexander Scriabin (1872-1915), Russian composer, wrote *Prometheus: The Poem of Fire* in 1910; Charles Tomlinson Griffes (1884-1920), American composer, wrote *The White Peacock* and *The Pleasure-Dome of Kubla Khan*.

Morte d'Oscar: Oscar Wilde died on November 30, 1900. He uttered the French phrase, which means "What does the glass matter, so long as one gets drunk," when playfully chided about the tawdriness of the hotel room in which he would later die.

Gottschalk in Peru: Louis Moreau Gottschalk (1829-1869), a New Orleans Creole, was the first internationally recognized American composer and pianist, partly because of his many tours in Europe and South America.

Burton on Fernando Po: Linguist and adventurer Richard Francis Burton (1821-1890), later knighted, traveled in disguise to Mecca, searched Africa for the Nile's source, then spent an unhappy Consulship on the island of Fernando Po before moving to better diplomatic posts.

Frozen Danube: Claudius Claudianus (c. AD 370-c. 406), Roman poet who praised the exploits of the Vandal/Roman general Stilicho (d. AD 408), especially in his battles against the Visigoth Alaric, who died soon after sacking Rome in AD 410.

Death of Caracalla: Caracalla, Roman Emperor (AD 211-217); Geta, Caracalla's brother, whom he murdered; Crassus, Roman Triumvir and general, slain by the Parthians at Carrhae in 53 BC with the loss of three legions; Elagabalus, Roman Emperor (AD 218-222).

Hadrian at Tivoli: Hadrian, Roman Emperor (AD 117-138), famous for his travels, his still-extant villa near Tivoli (Tibur), and his immoderate grief over the death of his friend and lover, Antinous, whom he had worshiped as a god throughout the Empire.

Trajan at the Persian Gulf: Trajan, Roman Emperor (AD 96-117), expanded the Roman Empire to its greatest extent, conquering what is now Iraq all the way to the Persian Gulf. Hadrian gave up this farthest eastern conquest because it could not be held.

Red Skeletons of Herculaneum: Herculaneum, town destroyed along with Pompeii by Mt. Vesuvius in AD 79. The skeletons found there are almost the only ones to survive from the Roman world since most "pagan" Romans cremated their dead. Some have a reddish cast.

Agrippina: Sister of the Emperor Caligula, niece and wife of the Emperor Claudius, mother of the Emperor Nero.

Caesar in Parthia: Julius Caesar had planned an invasion of Parthia (formerly Persia) shortly after the Ides of March, 44 BC. Ctesiphon was its capital. He sought glory but also wanted to avenge the defeat of Crassus (see "Death of Caracalla" note). Servilia, the domineering mother of Brutus, was Caesar's favorite mistress.

Clodia: Aristocratic, politically-astute mistress of the poet

Catullus, who called her "Lesbia."

Canto: "Kochab" is the orange star in the top front of the Little Dipper's bowl. The word means "star" in Hebrew, and Kochab was considered the North Star by the ancient Hebrews.

Larry Johnson

Larry Johnson was born in Natchez, Mississippi, in 1945 and grew up in Jackson. He attended Mississippi College for his B.A. and then the University of Arkansas, receiving his M.A. and M.F.A. Degrees in 1970. He has taught at Alma College, the University of New Orleans, North Carolina State University, and Louisburg College. He lives in Raleigh, North Carolina. In the fall of 2006 he gave a reading of his poems at the Library of Congress. *Veins* is his first published volume of poetry.

LaVergne, TN USA
25 February 2010
174222LV00004B/58/P